CW00739914

1799

Established

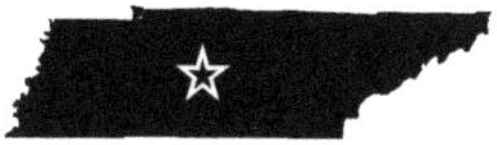

ATTRIBUTIONS
INTERIOR TEXT FONT | Minion Pro
COVER DESIGN & TYPESETTING | Robbie W. Grayson III
PHOTOGRAPHER | Jody Nash
EDITOR | Sharilyn S. Grayson

PUBLISHING INFORMATION
Traitmarker Media, LLC
www.traitmarkermedia.com
traitmarker@gmail.com
ISBN | 979-8-8689-2704-1

Our
TOWN

AN INSIDER'S GUIDE
TO FRANKLIN, TENNESSEE

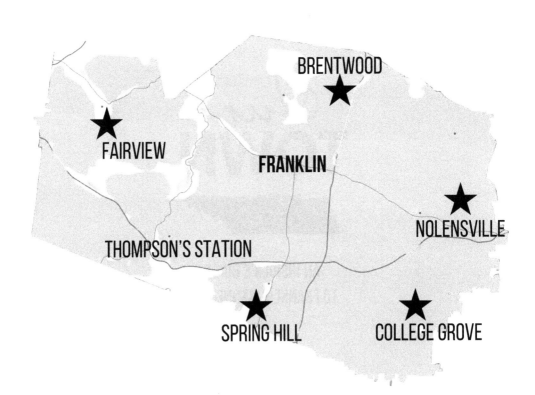

THE CITIES OF **WILLIAMSON COUNTY, TENNESSEE**

INVENTORY

Gray's on Main
MAIN STREET

Welcome!

What Is SISTER CITIES?

"Wild Daffodil"
Narcissus pseudonarcissus

Wild daffodils are known to bloom
in March for a few days before the next frost.

What is Sister Cities?

Sister Cities International was founded in 1956 by President Dwight D. Eisenhower as a nonpartisan 501(c)(3) nonprofit organization for the purpose of promoting peace through mutual respect, understanding, and cooperation—*one individual and one community at a time.* Our network unites tens of thousands of citizen diplomats and volunteers in almost 500 member communities with represents over 2,000 partnerships in more than 140 countries.

Our members work with each other as vital part in creating a more peaceful world through people-to-people exchanges and initiatives to mitigate the chance of potentially turbulent and unmanageable conflicts. Fostering bonds between people from different communities around the world is a proven strategy to dispense peace and prosperity for all. The value of face-to-face meetings and personal relationships across borders doesn't just change the lives of individuals, but it helps communities all over the world to thrive.

Sister Cities of
Franklin & Williamson County

Sister Cities of Franklin & Williamson County was founded in 2002 as an outgrowth of the Franklin-based organization Leadership Franklin. We currently have Sister Cities in Carleton Place, Ontario Canada, County Laois, Ireland, and Bad Soden am Taunus, Germany. Our organization exists to build global relationships through personal interactions, to share cultural and educational experiences, and to inspire the economic growth of our communities.

In light of the bridge-building we do between our Sister Cities, we are proud to provide this guide as a resource to enhance the experiences of both residents and tourists to Franklin and Williamson County. With a shared commitment to fostering global connections and cultural enrichment, Sister Cities of Franklin & Williamson County serves as a bridge between the diverse cultures that make up our Sister Cities network.

The Purpose of This Guide

For Residents, this guide offers an opportunity to delve into the rich history, hidden gems, and local treasures that define Franklin and Williamson County. From historical landmarks to customary behavior *Our Town: An Insider's Guide to Franklin, Tennessee* provides insights that deepen the connection to our hometown.

Tourists, too, will find valuable insights within these pages. As you explore our city and county, this guide offers a curated itinerary that captures the essence of our community's unique character, hopefully giving you a tailored roadmap to create unforgettable memories.

So, whether you're a lifelong resident or a first-time visitor, let this guide be your companion on a journey of discovery, inviting you to experience the heart and soul of Franklin and Williamson County.

Franklin Theatre
MAIN STREET

Publisher
NOTE

"Jonquil"
Narcissus jonquilla

Jonquils look similar to their daffodil cousins.
Jonquil petals are much rounder than daffodils.

I AM PROUD TO PRESENT *Our Town: An Insider's Guide to Franklin, Tennessee* and sincerely hope that it will serve as a valuable resource, helping both residents and visitors alike to explore our vibrant, historic city. It is, therefore, essential to clarify what this guidebook includes and does not include:

WHAT THIS GUIDEBOOK INCLUDES

- HISTORICAL HIGHLIGHTS | Our guidebook provides insights into the rich history of Franklin, showcasing its significance during the Civil War, its historic downtown district, and the many landmarks that speak to its past.

- LOCAL ATTRACTIONS | We include recommendations for popular attractions, cultural venues, parks, and more to help you make the most of your time in Franklin.

- PRACTICAL INFORMATION | We offer tips on local customs and other practicalities to ensure your time in Franklin is enjoyable and stress-free.

- CULTURAL SENSIBILITIES | We highlight the customs and manners of its residents that have contributed to preserving the rich history of Franklin as well as encouraging progress.

- COMMUNITY INFRASTRUCTURE | We offer a glimpse into the institutions and city amenities that Franklin offers its residents which has made Franklin a coveted place to live.

WHAT THIS GUIDEBOOK DOES NOT INCLUDE

- DETAILS OF OTHER WILLIAMSON COUNTY CITIES | Williamson County comprises the cities of Franklin, Nolensville, Brentwood, Thompson's Station, Spring Hill, Fairview, and College Grove. The scope of this focuses on the City of Franklin, especially it's downtown district.

- COMPREHENSIVE LISTINGS | While we strive to include a wide range of recommendations, it is impossible to list every establishment or event in Franklin. In focusing on Franklin and Williamson County's history, we have restricted listings accordingly. Be open to discovering hidden gems that may not be mentioned here.

- DINING AND CULINARY DELIGHTS | Our culinary scene includes many restaurants, cafes, and eateries that offer a taste of Southern hospitality and other cuisines.

- SHOPPING AND ENTERTAINMENT | Explore our charming boutiques, antique stores, and gift shops, and sample entertainment options that will keep you engaged throughout your stay.

- UP-TO-THE-MINUTE INFORMATION | Franklin is constantly evolving, and new businesses and events may emerge after the publication of this guidebook. We recommend checking online resources or consulting locals for the most current information.

- PERSONAL EXPERIENCES | While we aim to provide a comprehensive overview, experiences can vary. The opinions and recommendations in this guidebook are based on research and expert insights, but your personal experiences may differ.

- IN-DEPTH HISTORICAL ANALYSIS | While we touch on the historical significance of Franklin, this guidebook does not provide exhaustive historical analysis. If you're a history enthusiast, consider delving deeper with additional resources.

The City of Franklin, Tennessee, has a wealth of experiences waiting for you to discover, and our guidebook is designed to be your trusted companion on this journey. We hope that it enhances your visit, allowing you to explore the city's unique charm, culture, and history.

Enjoy!

Robbie Grayson III | *Publisher*
TRAITMARKER MEDIA, LLC

Natchez Trace
BRIDGE

Connecting
COMMUNITIES

"Southern Magnolia Blossom"
Magnolia grandiflora

These giant magnolia blossoms are fragile,
Their smell has been described to that of Chanpagne.

SISTER CITIES OF FRANKLIN & WILLIAMSON COUNTY is a dynamic community volunteer organization that fosters personal connections and nurtures meaningful friendships between global communities. With a mission to bridge cultures, promote understanding, and encourage collaboration, the organization brings the world closer to the charming city of Franklin and its surrounding county.

Through a network of Sister Cities, Sister Cities serves as a cultural catalyst, facilitating exchanges, educational initiatives, and cross-cultural experiences. By connecting residents, students, and businesses with counterparts in Sister Cities, the organization creates opportunities for personal growth, mutual learning, and the sharing of diverse perspectives.

From art exhibitions to educational programs, from business collaborations to community events, Franklin and Williamson County Sister Cities continually seeks to strengthen the bonds of international friendship. By celebrating the richness of global diversity, we bring what is best and richest in our small town to the world stage, and we welcome the international contributions that make Franklin a better place. Along the way, we form friendships that enrich the lives of all who participate.

Join us as we celebrate the vibrant spirit of cultural exchange and forge lasting connections that transcend borders and create a world that is united in diversity.

About FRANKLIN

"TEXAS BLUEBONNETS"
Lupinus texensis

These beautiful flowers are not native to Tennessee,
and have likely migrated here because of eager, amateur gardeners.

FRANKLIN, TENNESSEE, a captivating city just south of Nashville and the county seat of Williamson County, strikes a harmonious balance between history and contemporary life. With a population of around 85,000, Franklin's charming historic downtown exudes Southern nostalgia through its preserved antebellum architecture, quaint Victorian styling, and welcoming businesses. Its Civil War heritage still resonates through sites like Carnton and Carter House, which bear witness to the tragedy of the Battle of Franklin.

Today, Franklin thrives as a cultural hub. Music flows through its veins, from local live music performances to events like the Pilgrimage Music & Cultural Festival. Culinary excellence reigns, with innovative twists on Southern cuisine at acclaimed eateries and a bustling farmers' market showcasing fresh produce.

Nature envelops Franklin, inviting outdoor exploration. Soft hills, gentle waterways, and lovely parks create a serene backdrop. Wide, safe sidewalks make a day's stroll a pleasure, and for hikers, the Natchez Trace Parkway connects to the Appalachian Trail. The Williamson County Performing Arts Center and Heritage Foundation show the city's commitment to education and culture.

However, its genuine hospitality is what defines Franklin. A warm community spirit infuses daily life, welcoming newcomers with open arms. Franklin, Tennessee, stands as a testament to the art of balancing a storied past with a vibrant present, a place where history and modernity dance in harmony, and where every corner tells a story of a city that embraces the future while cherishing its roots.

FORT GRANGER

In the spring of 1863, Federal forces commanded by Maj. Gen. Gordon Granger occupied Franklin. Construction of major fortifications began under the direction of Capt. W. E. Merrill, U.S. Corps of Engineers, the largest of them being placed on Figuers Bluff, 2 of a mile north on the Harpeth River. Fort Granger commanded the southern and northern approaches to Franklin and was adjacent to the critically important Tenn. & Ala. Railroad bridge. The artillery within the fort saw action twice in 1863 against Confederate cavalry forces. During the Battle of Franklin, Nov. 30, 1864, the site served as Hqtrs. of Maj. Gen. John M. Schofield (commander of U.S. forces) and as an active artillery position.

Pinkerton Park
NEAR FORT GRANGER

Fox & Locke
THE "OLD PUCKETT'S"

Getting
ACQUAINTED

"CROWN FLOWER"
Calotropis Gigantea

This flower is also called "milkweed"
and is, therefore, a weed.

FRANKLIN, TENNESSEE has a remarkably complex history that has shaped the way the city looks and feels. The following significant historic events have taken place in Franklin, Tennessee, and we hope that knowing about them gives you a sense of appreciation as you live or visit here.

HARPETH RIVER

Vital to any town is a good water supply, and ours is the Harpeth River, which you can see at Bicentennial Park, off the Mack Hatcher bridge, and at the edge of Pinkerton Park. At Franklin, the course of the river turns more northwesterly. A few miles northwest of Franklin is the mouth of one of the Harpeth's main tributaries, the West Harpeth, which drains much of the southern portion of Williamson County. Near this site is an antebellum plantation house called Meeting of the Waters. The river in this area flows quite near the Natchez Trace (the original road of that name, not the modern Parkway named for it, which is several miles distant). The river crosses into Davidson County and receives the flow of the Little Harpeth River, another important tributary. The stream flows near the unincorporated Nashville suburb of Bellevue and then continues into Cheatham County.

FOUNDING OF FRANKLIN
1799

Founded in 1799, our town was named after Benjamin Franklin. Ewen Cameron, a Scottish immigrant, was the first to build a log cabin here in 1798, just two years after Tennessee gained statehood. The founder of the town was Abram Maury, Jr., and Maury County, just south of us, takes its name from him. He purchased the land on which Franklin lies, and he laid out the town and filed the plan with the county clerk. The first settlers of Franklin were mostly Virginians. Our county archives building, located just off Main Street, tells the story of the founding of Franklin and its important historic moments through a series of artifacts and exhibits.

Franklin Masonic Hall Built
1823

The Masonic Hall, a notable historic building, was constructed for meetings and community events. The Masonic Hall of Hiram Masonic Lodge No. 7 is a historic Gothic revival building on South 2nd Avenue in Franklin, Tennessee. Constructed in 1823, it is the oldest public building in Franklin. It is nationally significant as the site of negotiations leading to the Treaty of Franklin, the first Indian removal treaty agreed after passage of the 1830 Indian Removal Act. It was declared a National Historic Landmark in 1973. It continued to serve the local Masonic lodge until its recent closure for renovation.

St. Paul's Episcopal Church
August 25, 1827

St. Paul's Episcopal Church was founded on August 25, 1827 in a room of the Hiram Masonic Lodge #7 in Franklin, Tennessee. Those persons "friendly to the formation of an Episcopal church in the area" met under the leadership of Reverend James Hervey Otey, who not only started this "Mother Church of the Diocese of Tennessee" but was also instrumental in starting several other churches and educational institutions in the area. He would later become the state's first bishop, as well as the bishop of Louisiana, Mississippi, Arkansas, and Indian Territory (all at the same time!). The church edifice was not started until 1831. When completed in 1834, it was called a "three-decker" building, which included the nave, slave galleries, and undercroft. The original altar silver, presented by the Ladies of St. Paul's Church in 1834, is still in use today, and its stained glass windows are Tiffany glass.

CARTER HOUSE
1830

The Carter House, which would later serve as a witness to the Battle of Franklin, was built around 1830 by Fountain Branch Carter. By 1860 he was a wealthy farmer and owned twenty-eight slaves. On November 30, 1864, the Battle of Franklin engulfed the property, resulting in heavy casualties and significant damage to the house. Remarkably, the Carter House remains preserved with battle scars still visible on its walls as well as nearby outbuildings. Today, it stands as a poignant reminder of the conflict, offering visitors insight into the hardships faced by civilians during the war and the resilience of those who called it home.

FRANKLIN FEMALE SEMINARY
1832

One of the earliest places for education for women in Tennessee, the Franklin Female Seminary was founded in 1832 by the Hines family, settlers from North Carolina. This early educational institution for girls reflected the growing importance of female education in the early 19th century. It aimed to provide young women with a well-rounded education encompassing literature, arts, and moral values in addition to householding skills like needlework. Though expensive for the time, the academy accepted trade in lumber, farm produce, and labor as part of tuition. St. Paul's Episcopal Church in Franklin supported the Seminary.

Incorporation of Franklin as a City
1838

Further solidifying its role as a regional hub, Franklin, Tennessee, was officially incorporated as a city on October 26, 1838. That day, the Tennessee State Legislature passed the act that officially transitioned Franklin from a town to a city. This act outlined the city's boundaries, established its government structure, and provided for the election of city officials. Following the incorporation, Franklin established its municipal government. This included the election of a mayor and a board of aldermen. Today, the mayor and board of aldermen still make important decisions for the city, guiding it in the rapid development arising from prosperity and an influx of new residents.

Lotz House
1858

The Lotz House was built in 1858 by German immigrant Johann Albert Lotz. The frame Federal-style home also served as a business location and showpiece for his artistic skills. Lotz, who was a piano maker by trade, was also a woodworker. His craftsmanship can be seen in the house today. Though the Lotz House witnessed intense fighting during the Battle of Franklin in late 1864, it survived without major damage. It stands today as a preserved historic site, offering insight into the Civil War era and of those who emigrated to this country.

BATTLE OF TRIUNE
1862

On June 11, 1862, Confederate and Federal forces clashed in the Battle of Triune, a precursor to larger engagements in the area. Federal forces, led by General David S. Stanley, were trying to secure communication and supply lines in Middle Tennessee when they encountered Confederate cavalry commanded by General Nathan Bedford Forrest. Despite being outnumbered, Forrest's Confederate forces delayed and harassed the U. S. troops in a series of skirmishes and cavalry clashes. Ultimately, the battle ended inconclusively, with neither side gaining a significant advantage. The Battle of Triune was part of the wider campaigns in Tennessee and demonstrated the importance of controlling key transportation routes during the Civil War.

Hood's Tennessee Campaign
1864

A series of military engagements and movements in the larger context of the American Civil War, Hood's Tennessee Campaign of 1864 was pivotal in determining the outcome of the American Civil War. It involved Confederate General John Bell Hood's efforts to capture Nashville by disrupting Federal General John Schofield's movements toward the Tennessee capital. The campaign included battles at Spring Hill, Franklin, and Nashville. Hood's army suffered heavy losses, particularly in the disastrous Battle of Franklin, before being decisively defeated at the Battle of Nashville. The Federal victory at Nashville marked the end of Hood's threat in Tennessee, and contributed to the overall collapse of the Confederacy.

WINSTEAD HILL
1864

Nearly two miles south of Franklin is a long ridge line dominated by Winstead and Breezy Hills. From the crest of Winstead Hill, Confederate General John Bell Hood made the decision to launch a massive attack on the Federal defensive position just south of the town. After fierce fighting and heavy Confederate losses the U. S. Army, commanded by General John Schofield, withdrew across the Harpeth River and retreated to Nashville. Today you can retrace the route of the battle starting at Winstead Hill Park and proceeding north along Columbia Avenue into downtown Franklin.

Battle of Franklin
November 30, 1864

One of the bloodiest battles of the American Civil War, the Battle of Franklin was a brutal and pivotal engagement between Federal and Confederate forces. The battle claimed the lives of nearly 2,500 soldiers and almost 7,000 were wounded. Interpretive markers at Eastern Flank Battlefield Park and Carter Hill Battlefield Park details what happened on that fateful day. Although the Confederates briefly captured parts of the Federal defensive line, their costly attack ultimately failed. Carter House and Carnton were the most impacted by the battle and both are open to the public today. The Battle of Franklin was a tragic prelude to the decisive Battle of Nashville.

CARNTON
1864

Carnton was established by Randal McGavock around 1800 and he built a large, Federal-style brick home in 1826. John McGavock, the youngest son, took over the farming operation when his father died in 1843. The family became incredibly wealthy and owned forty-four slaves in 1860. Carnton was significantly impacted by the Battle of Franklin. The home served as a field hospital for hundreds of wounded Confederate soldiers. After the war the McGavock family set aside a small tract of land near their home where nearly 1,500 Confederate soldiers were re-buried.

LILLIE MILLS
1869

After the Civil War, Franklin rebuilt and expanded. One important new industry was a flour mill built by Joshua B. Lillie to process and export the grain grown by local farmers. Lillie Mills produced and transported Franklin Lady Flour and other products across the south. On the western edge of town near the railroad tracks, you can still see the massive, five-story grain elevator that stored products to be transported by train. The second largest grain elevator in the state, it was built by the new owners in 1926, and though it is unused today, it survived the fire that destroyed the mill in 1958. On Main Street, you can still see Lillie House, the stately Queen Anne mansion that Joshua Lillie bought with the profits from his mill.

BATTLE GROUND ACADEMY
1889

A private college preparatory school, Battleground Academy was founded in 1889 as a coeducational school by a group of local citizens. Initially established to provide education for the children of Civil War veterans, it aimed to promote academic excellence and character development. Over the years, it evolved into a prominent college preparatory institution, offering a comprehensive education program. The original 1889 building on the western edge of downtown houses the lower grades, while a new campus on Mack Hatcher Boulevard houses the upper grades. Battleground Academy has played a vital role in the Franklin community, emphasizing the values of scholarship, leadership, and service. It continues to be a respected educational institution in Tennessee.

THE DOWNTOWN POST OFFICE
1924

Built in 1924, the Franklin Post Office stands at Five Points, the intersection where Main Street meets Fifth Avenue and Columbia Pike. A federal government building until 1992, the post office became a Williamson County building when the county bought it and began leasing it to private operators. The basement housed valuable county documents, such as wills and deeds, until the county built a new library on Columbia Pike and transformed the old library into the county archives. The basement also provided office spaces and housed the Heritage Foundation for a time. After a temporary closure, new operators Matt and Julie Brown are reviving the old post office, keeping an important piece of Franklin History alive.

FOUNDING OF THE FACTORY
1929

In 1929, the people of Franklin bought stock in the Allen Manufacturing Company, allowing it to begin construction on a brick stoveworks factory at the west of town along the railroad. However, the company went bankrupt during the Great Depression, and Dortch Stove Works took over in 1932. The Factory was a thriving business and a vital employer for decades, changing hands to Magic Chef stoves and then Jamison Bedding. Then, in 1990, the last manufacturing pulled out, leaving the Factory dormant and falling to ruin. In 1996, local businessman Calvin LeHew purchased the building from the city and transformed it into a shopping, dining, and entertainment venue. Under new ownership, the Factory continues as a gathering place for Franklin, housing the local Farmer's Market and a number of charitable events in addition to its retail and dining spaces.

FRANKLIN THEATRE
1937

The iconic Franklin Theatre has a rich history dating back to its founding in 1937. A local businessman, Rogers Caldwell, recognized the need for a cultural and entertainment hub in the community during the Great Depression. The theater quickly became a beloved gathering place, hosting movies, live performances, and community events. Over the years, it underwent renovations and modernizations, ensuring its relevance in the changing entertainment landscape. Despite facing closure in the 2000s, the Franklin Theatre was lovingly restored and reopened in 2011, thanks to the dedicated efforts of preservationists and the community. Today, it continues to thrive, offering a lovely, vintage venue for theater, live music, comedy, films, and private events.

DESEGREGATION OF
FRANKLIN SPECIAL SCHOOL DISTRICT &
WILLIAMSON COUNTY SCHOOLS
1961 & 1967

During a time when African-American residents of Franklin, Tennessee made up one-third of its population, the Williamson County Committee of Christian Men (WCCCM) petitioned the County Court to act on six areas in which they wanted an extension of rights for the Black community. Desegregating Franklin schools was the first request. Within the same year, Franklin Special School District began desegregating its schools, starting with first grade. By the Fall of 1967, Williamson County School Board desegregated its schools. Today, Williamson County and Franklin Special School District schools provide excellent education.

Natchez Trace Parkway Bridge
1994

Traveling out of Franklin east toward the town of Fairview on Highway 96, motorists pass under the iconic white arches of the Natchez Trace Parkway Bridge. The Natchez Trace stretches from Nashville, Tennessee to Natchez, Mississippi, following the ancient game trails of migratory bison and other game and the paths of Native Americans who hunted them, following the "traces" of the animals. The cathedral arch bridge stands 145 feet tall and stretches just over 1,500 feet. It opened to the public in March 1994, and motorists enjoy the expansive view of the Williamson County countryside from the top as they cross.

Carnton

HISTORIC HOME

Exploring
DOWNTOWN

"WHITE CLOVER"
Trifolium repens

Honeybees and bumblebees love this flower.
Its leaves favor the shape of a shamrock, hence its name.

FRANKLIN, TENNESSEE, is a historic town with such a rich heritage and a charming downtown area that preservation efforts have not only saved many of its historic sites but have also made them available to the public. What follows are some of the most common and notable historic sites that you can find in Franklin.

HISTORIC DOWNTOWN FRANKLIN

Franklin maintains a picturesque downtown area with historic architecture, boutique shops, innovative restaurants, and a vibrant arts scene. The Downtown Franklin Association and its members preserve the history and charm of our community, support small business, build collaborative marketing campaigns, and host signature festivals and events each year. DFA membership is open for businesses and building owners located in the 16-block historic district in downtown Franklin. When you become a DFA member, you are also automatically a member of its parent organization, the Heritage Foundation of Williamson County.

P.O. Box 723
Franklin, TN 37065
www.downtownfranklintn.com
615.905.8937

Franklin Main Street

The heart of downtown, Main Street is known for its charming atmosphere, local businesses, regular events like the Franklin Art Scene, and festivals like the Main Street Festival, Pumpkinfest, and Dickens of a Christmas. Consider downtown Franklin's main thoroughfare a must-see attraction. It has been designated a Great American Main Street and is listed on the National Register of Historic Places. When you see all that Franklin's Main Street has to offer, you'll understand its appeal.

207 East Main Street
Franklin, TN 37064
www.downtownfranklintn.com
615-591-8500

FRANKLIN FIRST UNITED METHODIST CHURCH

The Franklin First United Methodist Church in Franklin, Tennessee, has a rich history dating back to 1810. It was established by early settlers, and its original log cabin structure has since evolved into a prominent place of worship in the community. During the Civil War, the church served as a hospital for wounded soldiers, reflecting its commitment to both faith and compassion. The current Gothic-style building was constructed in 1891 and stands as an architectural gem. Over the years, it has remained a spiritual and cultural center, dedicated to community service and worship. The Franklin First United Methodist Church continues to be an integral part of Franklin's heritage and religious life.

148 5th Avenue South
Franklin, TN 37064
www.franklinfumc.org
(615) 794-6626

Fourth Avenue Church of Christ

The Fourth Avenue Church of Christ in Franklin, Tennessee, established in 1833, it is one of the oldest congregations in the city. The church played a significant role in the Civil Rights Movement, as it was one of the first integrated churches in the area, promoting racial harmony during a tumultuous era. The historic building, dating back to 1882, has been a symbol of community and faith. Today, the Fourth Avenue Church of Christ continues to be a place of worship and a reminder of the importance of inclusivity and unity in the face of adversity.

117 4th Avenue North
Franklin, TN 37064
www.fourthavenue.church
(615) 794-6626

St. Phillip's Catholic Church

Fronting Main Street and stretching the block between First and Second Avenues, St. Phillip's Catholic Church was built by Irish Catholic railroad workers who arrived after the Civil War. Eager for a spiritual home of their own, the workers built the church by hand, even firing their own bricks on site. The original church structure, now a chapel beside the larger church, was finished in 1871, and in 1898, Father John Nolan built a rectory nearby, making the church a parish with a resident priest. In 1921, to commemorate the hundred years since the first private celebration of Mass in Williamson County, the ladies of the church contributed the beautiful stained glass panels.

113 2nd Avenue South
Franklin, TN 37064
www.stphilipfranklin.com
615.794.8588

McLemore House

The McLemore House is also known as the Harvey Mc-Lemore House, as it was the home of former slave Harvey McLemore, who became a successful farmer. Harvey McLemore was sold as "a slave for life" in 1859 to William S. McLemore, who was then the county clerk, and who later became a judge. In 1880, Harvey McLemore purchased four lots from Judge William S. McLemore and built his house as one of the first residences in the subdivision. Harvey was just the third African-American to purchase property in Hard Bargain. In 1998, the house was renovated for use as a museum. It is now a museum, the McLemore House African-American Museum or the McLemore House Museum.

446 11th Avenue North
Franklin, TN 37064
www.aahswc.org
615.790.0527

Franklin Theatre

The Franklin Theatre is a restored movie palace that opened in 1937. Though its doors closed in 2007 due to the recession, the Heritage Foundation, a nonprofit preservation group, purchased the historic landmark. In a period of three years and with an investment of more than $8 million, the Franklin Theater has been open to host live performances, concerts, films, and other events.

419 Main Street
Franklin, TN 37064
www.franklintheatre.com
615.538.2076

The Factory at Franklin

The Factory at Franklin is a former stoveworks factory built during the Great Depression and in continuous use until the 1990s. The City of Franklin bought the building in 1958 when its future was in jeopardy and leased it to Magic Chef and to Jameson Bedding. In 1996, visionary Franklin businessman Calvin LeHew purchased the derelict space and transformed it into a beautiful retail space and event venue.

230 Franklin Road
Franklin, TN 37064
www.factoryatfranklin.com
615.791.1777

CARNTON

A historic antebellum home that served as a field hospital during the Battle of Franklin in the Civil War, the house and grounds are now open for tours. Carnton, built in 1826, was one of the premier farms in Middle Tennessee. On November 30, 1864, the home and the McGavock family who lived there found themselves in the middle of one of the most dramatic events of the Civil War. The McGavock Confederate Cemetery was established by the family after the conclusion of the war.

1345 Eastern Flank Circle
Franklin, TN 37167
www.boft.org/carnton-history
615.794.0903

CARTER HOUSE

Another historic home that played a significant role in the Civil War and is now a museum open for guided tours is Carter House. Built in 1830, Carter House was the center of a successful farming operation by the time of the Civil War. On November 30, 1864, the home and the families who lived there found themselves in the middle of one of the most dramatic events of the Civil War.

1140 Columbia Avenue
Franklin, TN 37167
www.boft.org/carter-house-history
615.791.1861

Lotz House

A Civil War-era house museum with unique artifacts and a connection to the Battle of Franklin. The Lotz House (Lotz rhymes with "boats") is a two-story frame house built in 1858. The house is significant both for its craftsmanship and for being in the epicenter of the Battle of Franklin in the American Civil War in 1864.

1111 Columbia Avenue
Franklin, TN 37064
www.lotzhouse.com
615.790.7190

Gentry Farm

Gentry Farm in Franklin, Tennessee, was originally a land grant property in the 19th century that evolved into a working farm. In recent years, Gentry Farm has transitioned into an event venue and educational space that is only open a few days a year, allowing visitors to experience a slice of rural life and learn about farming practices. This transformation highlights the importance of preserving historical farmland and sharing its legacy with the community, making Gentry Farm a unique and educational destination in Franklin. The farm was the home of the late Jimmy Gentry whom locals affectionately called "Coach". Coach was an infantry solider in World War I, serving in the 42 Rainbow Division in which he was a liberator of the Dachau Concentration Camp in Bavaria, Germany.

1974 New Highway 96 West
Franklin, TN 37064
www.gentryfarm.com
615.794.4368

Historic Franklin Presbyterian Church

The original church on this site was established in 1842. It caught on fire in 1905 and suffered severe damage. While the original stained-glass windows were destroyed by the fire, the current windows are faithful reproductions of those designs, and the original church pews, which were rescued by those early congregants during the fire, are still used in the sanctuary today. The original bell is still operational and hanging in the current bell tower.

435 Main Street
Franklin, TN 37064
www.historicfranklinpc.org
615.794.9094

Leiper's Fork

Known for its artistic community, antique shops, and scenic countryside, Leiper's Fork is an unincorporated rural village located 15 minutes from downtown Franklin in Williamson County, Tennessee. As one of the only towns located directly on the historic Natchez Trace Parkway, the village has been named to the National Register of Historical Places. Roughly an hour south of Nashville, this creative and rustic village has become a favorite spot for locals and tourists alike.

4140 Old Hillsboro Road
Franklin, TN 37064
www.visitleipersforktn.com

Winstead Hill Park

A park offering panoramic views of the Civil War battlefield and the surrounding area, Winstead Hill in Franklin, Tennessee forms part of the 1864 Battle of Franklin battlefield. A circle of flags atop the hill represents the different divisions which fought in the battle of Franklin. Winstead Hill is a U.S. National Historic Landmark area. In the battle, Confederate troops under General Hood attacked from Winstead Hill.

4023 Columbia Avenue
Franklin, TN 37064
www.franklintn.gov
615.794.2103

Pinkerton Park

Pinkerton Park, located on Murfreesboro Road, is the most highly used passive park in the park system. The Harpeth River flows along the west side of the park, while Fort Granger lies to the north. Tinkerbell playground, with playground equipment for children, is located near the pavilions. Three picnic pavilions provide a total of 14 sheltered tables in addition to nine other picnic tables and grills strategically placed throughout the park. A one-mile paved pedestrian track encompasses the entire park. The Sue Douglas Berry Memorial pedestrian bridge connects the downtown area with Pinkerton Park. Two of the pavilions at Pinkerton Park are available for rent.

405 Murfreesboro Road
Franklin, TN 37064
www.franklintn.gov
615.794.2103

Harlinsdale Farm

A 198-acre historic horse farm with green spaces and trails, Harlinsdale houses the annual Pilgrimage Music & Cultural Festival and the Franklin Fourth of July celebration. Harlinsdale Farm was listed on the National Register of Historic Places in 2006. It dates from 1933, when WW Harlin bought it to join the Tennessee Walking Horse industry. Its main horse stable, the centerpiece of the property, was completed in 1935, and the farm produced champion horse Midnight Sun.

239 Franklin Road
Franklin, TN 37064
www.franklintn.gov
615.794.2103

Franklin Farmers Market

A seasonal market offering locally grown produce, artisan products, and crafts, the Franklin Farmers Market is a true Tennessee farmers market. From produce, fruit, and dairy to baked goods and meats, you'll find delicious fresh food at the Franklin Farmers Market. And because it's all from local farms, the variety of goods increases and changes each week through the seasons. You can taste the difference, because it all comes straight from the farm to the market, ripe and ready to enjoy. It's Tennessee farm fresh food from real farmers, every Saturday morning at the Franklin Farmers Market. Plus, a select number of local crafts persons at the market create unique and beautiful goods for you to enjoy.

230 Franklin Road
Franklin, TN 37064
www.franklinfarmersmarket.com
615.592.1337

Williamson County Ag Expo Park

A venue for various events, including rodeos, fairs, and agricultural exhibitions, the Ag Expo Park has been thoughtfully designed to host a variety of activities including trade shows, agricultural events, and everything in between. With over 45 major events per year, it has become a popular destination for local, regional, and national events. Located directly off the mezzanine with 4,050 square feet, its meeting room comfortably seats up to 300 guests and can be used for banquets, meetings, seminars, or additional vendor space. It can be rented independently or in conjunction with main arena events.

4215 Long Lane
Franklin, TN 37064
www.williamsoncounty-tn.gov
615.595.1227

McGavock Confederate Cemetery

A burial site for Confederate soldiers near Carnton, the McGavock Confederate Cemetery was established in June 1866 as a private cemetery on land donated by the McGavock planter family. The nearly 1,500 Confederate soldiers buried there were casualties of the Battle of Franklin that took place November 30, 1864. Union soldiers also honorably rest in peace at the site.

Confederate Cemetery
Franklin, TN 37064
www.mcgavockcemetery.org

Fort Granger

A Civil War fortification offering panoramic views of the town, Fort Granger is one of several fortifications constructed in the Franklin Battlefield. The fort was built in 1862 and used by Union troops to defend their positions in Middle Tennessee against Confederate attackers. The Second Battle of Franklin in 1864, part of the Franklin-Nashville Campaign in the Western Theater, was the most notable engagement of this area during the Civil War. Today, Fort Granger's remaining earthworks are preserved within a city park that is located near the center of Franklin. Fort Granger was named after Union General Gordon Granger who on June 19, 1865 notified the people of Texas that all enslaved peoples were free.

113 Fort Granger Drive
Franklin, TN 37064
www.franklintn.gov
615.794.2103

Gallery 202

An art gallery featuring local and regional artists' work, Gallery 202 is a diverse art gallery located in downtown Franklin, TN. As one of the premier art galleries in Franklin, we are dedicated to the art lover and collector. We offer an array of artistic styles and mediums including: Paintings, Antiques, Glass, Jewelry, Pottery, and Sculpture.

202 2nd Avenue South
Franklin, TN 37064
www.gallery202art.com
615.472.1134

Franklin Public Square

The center of downtown with a park-like setting, historic courthouse, and seasonal events. The Downtown Franklin Association and its members are dedicated to preserving the history and charm of our community, supporting small business, building collaborative marketing campaigns, and hosting signature festivals and events each year. DFA membership is open for businesses and building owners located in the 16-block historic district in downtown Franklin. When you become a DFA member, you are also automatically a member of its parent organization, the Heritage Foundation of Williamson County, TN.

Public Square
Franklin, TN 37064
wwwdowntownfranklintn.com
615.905.8937

The O'More College Mansion

The O'More College Mansion, originally built in 1903, served as a private residence for the prominent Carton family. In 1970, it was transformed into O'More College of Design, a renowned institution for art and design education where it remained an educational hub until 2018 when it merged with Belmont University. The Heritage Foundation of Williamson County recently purchased the property back from Belmont University and has renamed it Franklin Grove Estate & Gardens where it will preserve the charm of the local area. The main house on the former college campus is called the Abbey Leix Mansion (also known as the Winstead House) which pays homage to the Irish roots of the O'More family name which hails from Abbey Leix, Ireland, which is a city in County Laois, Ireland, one of Franklin's Sister Cities.

423 S Margin Street
Franklin, TN 37064
www.belmont.edu/omore
615.794.4254

WILLIAMSON COUNTY ARCHIVES AND MUSEUM

The Franklin Archives in Franklin, Tennessee, is a vital repository of the city's historical records and artifacts. Established to preserve the rich heritage of this community, it houses an extensive collection of documents, photographs, and memorabilia, dating back to Franklin's earliest days. This valuable resource serves as a window into the past, allowing residents and researchers to explore the city's development, notable events, and the lives of its inhabitants. The Franklin Archives plays a crucial role in education, fostering an understanding of the area's history, and ensuring that the legacy of Franklin, Tennessee, is cherished and passed down to future generations.

611 West Main Street
Franklin, TN 37064
www.williamsoncounty-tn.gov
(615) 790-5462

Puckett's Restaurant

Puckett's Restaurant in Franklin, Tennessee, is a quintessential Southern dining experience. Housed in a historic building, it exudes rustic charm and offers a delectable taste of traditional Southern cuisine. Guests can indulge in classics like hot chicken, fried catfish, and mouthwatering barbecue, while enjoying live music performances that celebrate the city's musical heritage. The warm, inviting atmosphere and friendly service make it a local favorite. Puckett's commitment to showcasing regional flavors and fostering a sense of community through food and music has established it as a beloved institution in Franklin, serving up a slice of authentic Tennessee culture.

120 4th Avenue South
Franklin, TN 37064
www.puckettsgro.com
(615) 794-5527

Grays on Main

Grays on Main is a historic gem in downtown Franklin, Tennessee, housed in a 19th-century building with a rich history. Originally a pharmacy, it later served as a performing arts venue and a restaurant. Today, Grays on Main combines the best of the past and present, offering a unique dining and entertainment experience. The restaurant's upscale Southern cuisine features modern twists on classic dishes. With its vintage decor and live music, it pays homage to its heritage while creating a vibrant contemporary atmosphere. Grays on Main has become a cherished establishment, known for preserving the town's history while serving up delicious food and entertainment.

332 Main Street
Franklin, TN 37064
www.graysonmain.com
(615) 435-3603

Kimbro's Pickin' Parlor

Kimbro's Pickin Parlor is a charming and intimate music venue nestled in historic downtown Franklin, Tennessee. This beloved spot offers an authentic taste of the region's rich musical heritage. With its rustic decor, cozy atmosphere, and a stage that has hosted countless talented musicians, it's a hub for bluegrass, country, and folk enthusiasts. Patrons can savor Southern cuisine and libations while tapping their toes to live performances or even join in the jam sessions. Kimbros Pickin Parlor embodies the soul of Tennessee's music scene, making it a must-visit for anyone seeking a genuine taste of the state's musical culture.

214 S Margin Street
Franklin, TN 37064
www.legendarykimbros.com

(615) 567-3877

The Red Barn
ON HILLSBORO ROAD

Community
SERVICES

"WILD MINT"
Mentha arvensis

Also called "field mint", this plant
flavors the drinks and foods of local cuisine.

PART OF WHAT MAKES FRANKLIN, TENNESSEE such a great place to live is the range of community services it makes available to support its residents. While the availability of specific services evolve over time, what follows are some of the most common community services that Franklin residents enjoy.

Public Safety Services

The Williamson County Public Safety Administration seeks out joint opportunities, helps the community overcome obstacles and assists with daily operations. We are working daily to serve our communities and citizens more effectively and efficiently. Emergencies occur on large and small scales. From flooding and tornadoes to roadway incidents and cyberattacks, emergencies arise with little to no warning. The best way to prepare for any disaster lies with each individual citizen. After disasters, assistance sometimes becomes available from local, state, or even the federal government, but not always. You are your best and fastest option to recovering from a disaster! We are located at 304 Beasley Dr, Franklin, TN, 37064.

Law Enforcement

A dynamic community of 42 square miles and 84,454 residents, Franklin, located in the heart of Williamson County, has earned a national reputation as a safe and vibrant community. The Franklin Police Department, the ninth largest in the State, continues to maintain one of the lowest crime rates per capita in Tennessee. As the City continues to grow, we are constantly seeking new ways to exceed the needs and expectations of our residents. Keep an eye out for our famous dancing policeman, David Collins, who directs traffic with enthusiasm outside the Franklin Farmers Market Saturday mornings and at various church services on Sunday mornings.

Fire Department

Williamson Fire-Rescue, the partnership between the volunteer fire departments and Williamson County Government, is charged with ensuring that those who work, live, and play in Williamson County are served and protected by a professional, proficient, and progressive fire service system. Fire protection in the unincorporated areas of Williamson County, including Thompson's Station, is provided by three volunteer departments and one combination paid/volunteer fire department in Nolensville. Combined, these departments consist of fourteen stations. These are fully staffed with volunteer firefighters who have trained and worked together to provide the best service at any given time.

EDUCATION SERVICES

The Williamson County School District and Franklin Special School District in Franklin, Tennessee, collectively serve the educational needs of the community. The Williamson County School District encompasses a large area, offering a high standard of education to a growing student population. Known for its academic excellence and numerous extracurricular opportunities, it consistently ranks among the top districts in the state. The Franklin Special School District, more focused on the city of Franklin, is equally dedicated to providing quality education and fostering student success. Both districts benefit from community support and a commitment to educational advancement, making them integral components of Franklin's thriving education system.

Libraries

Williamson County Public Library's (WCPL) Main Library is located on Columbia Avenue one mile south of historic downtown Franklin, Tennessee. The Main Library was organized in 1937, and the current facility opened in 2003. The library offers services like computer use, internet access, programs for teens, a book club, children's story hour, a kid's summer reading program, tax preparation, and many other clubs and programs. The beautiful building has a domed reading room upstairs, as well as many comfortable and attractive spaces to read and study.

Healthcare Services

Hospitals and Clinics: Medical facilities in Franklin provide state of the art healthcare services, from primary care to specialized treatments. Our Public Health Department specializes in health promotion, disease prevention, and community health programs. Williamson Medical center, an outstanding hospital with a recently renovated emergency room, serves the county from a central location off I-65.

Parks & Recreation Services

The Parks Department within the City of Franklin maintains over 900 acres of park land divided into 18 parks, including passive parks, active parks, and historical parks. Each park has its own character and amenities. Walking and fitness trails, playgrounds, picnic tables and shelter areas, sports fields, skateboarding, disc golf, tennis, basketball and fishing, are a few of the possible park features. Specific pavilions and facilities are also available to rent for a reasonable fee for your personal or corporate functions.

Social Services

Williamson County and Franklin Tennessee charities, churches, and government DHS social service agencies offer emergency financial help or free supplies to low-income or struggling families, who can also get help with paying electric bills or rent, or maybe a free bag of food or clothes. Other assistance in Williamson County ranges from budgeting and debt relief to job programs, back to school supplies, and free transportation. Franklin and Williamson County families can also look into healthcare resources, as too many families are uninsured. They can find free dental care, eye exams nearby, or prescription drugs. There are also other resources for children, ranging from CHIP medical care to free Christmas gifts.

Community Development

The Community Development Division is responsible for ensuring that property development within the unincorporated county occurs in a manner that attempts to preserve the character of the essentially rural community, while accommodating record growth. This is accomplished with a strong, award-winning, performance-based Zoning Ordinance and through coordination with various federal, state, and local stakeholders. Within Williamson County government, specialized departments like Building Codes, Code Compliance, Engineering, Planning & Zoning, and Sewage Disposal play key roles in achieving goals.

TRANSPORTATION SERVICES

Franklin Transit connects people in the Franklin and Cool Springs area by providing convenient transit service to downtown Franklin, Cool Springs, Columbia State, Williamson Medical Center, Fieldstone Farms, Independence Square, Franklin High School, and many Franklin neighborhoods. Display panels in lobbies of local businesses and hotels along with a robust mobile app help transit riders locate buses and arrival/departure times. The service is managed and operated by the TMA Group for the Franklin Transit Authority. The TMA Group in accordance with Title VI of the Civil Rights Act of 1964 assures "no person shall, on the grounds of race, color or national origin, be excluded from participation in, be denied the benefits of, or be subjected to discrimination under any program or activity receiving federal financial assistance."

Environmental Services

The Sanitation and Environmental Services Department is responsible for the collection and disposal of municipal solid waste, curbside recycling, residential yard and bulk waste, and city-approved containers within Franklin city limits. Our mission is to provide the citizens of Franklin effective and efficient solid waste service in an environmentally and economically responsible manner.

Downtown Franklin Art Crawl

The Franklin Downtown Art Crawl in Franklin, Tennessee, is a vibrant and community-oriented event celebrating the local arts scene. Held regularly in the historic downtown district, it provides a platform for local and regional artists to showcase their talents. Attendees can explore a diverse range of artwork, from paintings and sculptures to photography and crafts, often displayed in various galleries, boutiques, and public spaces. The Art Crawl fosters a lively, creative atmosphere, with opportunities to engage with artists and purchase unique pieces. It not only supports the arts but also enriches the cultural fabric of Franklin, making it a must-visit for art enthusiasts and a testament to the city's thriving artistic community.

COMMUNITY SUPPORT SERVICES

Our City is a bustling community where people come to live, work and play. Customer service is our top priority. In accordance with the requirements of Title II of the Americans with Disabilities Act of 1990, the City of Franklin, TN (City) will not discriminate against any qualified individuals with disabilities on the basis of disability in the City's services, programs, or activities.

Animal Services

The Williamson County Animal Shelter in Franklin, Tennessee, is a compassionate haven for animals in need. This modern, well-equipped facility is dedicated to the welfare of animals in the community. It provides shelter, medical care, and opportunities for adoption, striving to find loving homes for countless pets. The shelter also offers educational programs and promotes responsible pet ownership. Staffed by dedicated professionals and volunteers, it plays a vital role in addressing animal welfare issues in Williamson County. By offering support, advocacy, and a safe haven for animals, the Williamson County Animal Shelter exemplifies the community's commitment to the well-being of its four-legged residents.

CIVIC ENGAGEMENT SERVICES

On August 19, 2020, Franklin, Tennessee was recognized today as one of 10 All-America City award winners. The National Civic League presented this honor to recognize Franklin's work in inclusive civic engagement to address health and well-being and create stronger connections among residents, businesses and nonprofit and government leaders. Franklin has reckoned with its past while preparing for a healthy future by: adding plaques about the city's African American history to the town square; the City partnered with Franklin Tomorrow with hosting a series of 'On The Table' civic conversations; and getting healthy with 'Get Fit Franklin. Franklin Tomorrow worked with the City in pursuing this award. Their inclusive approach to addressing the past and planning for the future can be seen in their featured projects.

GRACEWORKS

GraceWorks is a prominent nonprofit organization in Franklin, TN, dedicated to providing essential assistance and support to individuals and families facing hardship. With a mission rooted in compassion, GraceWorks offers a wide array of services, including food assistance, financial aid, job training, and access to healthcare. They operate a food pantry, thrift store, and educational programs to empower their clients towards self-sufficiency. GraceWorks plays a vital role in the community, addressing the needs of those struggling with hunger, homelessness, and financial instability. Their commitment to fostering a sense of grace and empowerment in the lives of the people they serve makes them an invaluable resource in Franklin.

Smalltown
WISDOM

"COMMON DANDELION"
Taraxacum officinale

The dandelion is a hardy plant that puts up well
with the extreme heat of Williamson County.

WHILE MANY THINGS HAVE CHANGED over time in Franklin, Tennessee, what has not changed is the small town wisdom that governs the relationships among residents in business, church, civic engagements, and everyday life. If you pay close attention, you will see not only that it's true but that there's a great benefit from taking it into consideration.

"Kindness Is Contagious"

A simple act of kindness can create a ripple effect, spreading goodwill throughout the community. When Southerners say, "Kindness Is Contagious," they're emphasizing the cultural value of hospitality and goodwill. Acts of kindness and friendliness can inspire others to respond with generosity and warmth. In Franklin, we enjoy spreading positivity and creating a harmonious and supportive community. The simple acts of kindness that have a profound impact on individuals and can then impact society as a whole.

"Neighbors Are Family"

Treating your neighbors with care and respect fosters a strong sense of unity and support. When Southerners say, "Neighbors Are Family," they're expressing the strong sense of community and closeness that characterizes the importance of relationships and connections in Southern culture. People in the South often treat their neighbors with the same care, respect, and support that they would extend to family members. In Franklin, your neighbors often bring a casserole when you're sick, volunteer to help you move, or mow your lawn when you get busy. The bonds formed among neighbors ensure that people look out for each other, offer help in times of need, and create a tight-knit network within their communities that feels like extended family.

"Slow Down & Enjoy Life"

Embrace the slower pace of small town living, and take the time to appreciate life's simple pleasures. When Southerners say, "Slow Down & Enjoy Life," they are encouraging a more relaxed and unhurried approach to life. The Southern lifestyle values taking the time to savor moments, appreciate simple pleasures, and prioritize personal connections. We avoid the stress and rush of modern life and instead focus on living in the moment, cherishing traditions, and finding contentment in the unhurried pace of Southern living. This saying embodies a cultural philosophy of finding joy and fulfillment in the quieter, more leisurely aspects of life.

"Front Porch Talks Matter"

Engaging in conversations on front porches or side-walks builds bonds that go beyond digital interactions. When Southerners say, "Front Porch Talks Matter," they highlight the significance of informal conversations and social gatherings on the front porch. There is a real importance to community, storytelling, and interpersonal connections. Front porch talks are a tradition where neighbors, friends, and family come together to share stories, offer support, and build relationships. Southern culture emphasizes hospitality and fostering meaningful connections through open, relaxed, and face-to-face communication, acknowledging that these moments of bonding can be profound and meaningful in building strong, interconnected communities.

"History Connects Us"

Valuing local history helps preserve traditions, maintains a sense of continuity, and "scales" growth. When Southerners say, "History Connects Us," they are emphasizing the deep-rooted connection between the past and the present in Southern culture. Traditions, heritage, and shared experiences tie communities together over time. Southerners often take pride in their history, both the triumphs and challenges, as it forms the backdrop to their identity and sense of belonging. This saying signifies that an understanding of history helps strengthen bonds, preserve cultural values, and provide a sense of continuity among Southerners.

"A Helping Hand Goes Far"

Offering assistance to others in times of need strengthens the fabric of the community. When Southerners say, "A Helping Hand Goes Far," they emphasize the value of kindness, generosity, and community support. Offering assistance and support to others, especially in times of need, benefits not only the recipient but the giver. It also contributes to the strength and cohesion of the whole community. This saying underscores the Southern culture of neighborly care and the value of simple acts of goodwill.

"Lend a Listening Ear"

Being there for someone to share stories and concerns builds trust and friendship. When Southerners say, "Lend a Listening Ear," they are emphasizing the importance of attentive and empathetic listening in building relationships and providing support. In Franklin, we value being there for others in times of joy or distress and offering a compassionate and nonjudgmental ear to share their thoughts, concerns, and stories. This saying reflects the Southern culture's value of genuine connections, where people express care and understanding through the act of active listening, fostering a sense of belonging, trust, and community support.

"Nature Heals"

Despite the humid heat of summer (or the freezing cold of our long winters), spending time outdoors, enjoying the beauty of nature, can bring solace and rejuvenation. When Southerners say, "Nature Heals," they highlight the therapeutic and rejuvenating power of spending time in the natural world. We believe that connecting with nature can provide solace, tranquility, and a sense of well-being. This saying embodies the Southern appreciation for outdoor activities like gardening, fishing, barbecuing, swimming, or simply enjoying the beauty of the landscape. It emphasizes the healing qualities of the environment, both physical and emotional, and underscores the idea that communing with nature can offer a profound sense of peace and restoration.

"Embrace Newcomers"

Welcoming newcomers ensures that the community remains diverse, vibrant, and open-minded. It also assures that newcomers have opportunities to assimilate into our small-town values. When Southerners say, "Embrace Newcomers," they promote a welcoming and inclusive attitude toward people who are new to the community. Southern culture is hospitable and warm, encouraging established residents to be open, friendly, and supportive toward those who have recently arrived. This saying reflects the belief that fostering connections and showing kindness to newcomers not only enriches the community but also preserves the tradition of Southern hospitality, making everyone feel valued and part of the local culture.

"Celebrate Together"

Franklin & Williamson County offer myriad opportunities for the community to "fellowship". Coming together for festivals and events creates cherished memories and strengthens bonds. When Southerners say, "Celebrate Together," they emphasize the significance of communal gatherings and shared festivities. In the South, we love coming together to celebrate, whether it's a holiday, a local event, or simply the joys of life. Celebrating as a community strengthens bonds, creates cherished memories, and fosters a sense of belonging. It embodies the spirit of hospitality and togetherness, where people find joy in each other's company and make any moment special through shared laughter, food, and traditions.

"Simplicity is Elegance"

Embracing a simple lifestyle encourages authenticity and reduces unnecessary stress. When a Southerner says, "Simplicity Is Elegance," they emphasize the idea that understated, uncomplicated, and genuine aspects of life hold their own beauty and charm. It reflects the Southern culture's appreciation for the unpretentious, where less can be more, and modesty is valued. This saying underscores the belief that elegance is not necessarily found in extravagance, but rather in the purity of simplicity, whether in manners, hospitality, or the pleasures of everyday life. It reflects a sense of grace and refinement that arises from authenticity and a focus on what truly matters.

"Respect Tradition, Embrace Change"

Honoring tradition while being open to innovation ensures a balanced and thriving community. When a Southerner says, "Respect Tradition, Expect Change," they recognize the importance of honoring their cultural heritage and values while embracing progress and evolution. It signifies a balanced approach to life, acknowledging that while tradition and heritage provide a strong foundation, adaptation and innovation are also essential. This saying reflects the Southern culture's ability to cherish its roots and history while remaining open to new ideas and embracing societal shifts. It embodies a sense of resilience, where the past informs the present, but change is welcomed as a means of growth and improvement.

Carter House
ON COLUMBIA AVENUE

Neighborly
MANNERS

"Lamb's Ear"
Stachys byzantina

This adorable plant lives up to its name
with the soft texture of a lamb's ear.

"Small town" manners in Franklin, Tennessee, because we are a Southern town, are characterized by a strong sense of hospitality, politeness, and community-oriented values. Residents of Franklin take pride in their traditional Southern manners, which reflect a genuine warmth and friendliness in their interactions. What follows are twelve manners that are valued in Franklin.

Warm Greetings

In Franklin, people often greet each other with a smile, a nod, or a friendly "hello." It's common to acknowledge strangers and acquaintances alike with a kind word or a simple gesture. "Warm greetings" to a Southerner from Franklin, Tennessee, mean offering a sincere and friendly welcome to others. Southerners, in general, are known for their hospitality and politeness. In Franklin, we stop to give directions, say good morning, or pet your dog. We use polite language, make eye contact, and offer a genuine smile when meeting someone new or even when welcoming friends and family. Southerners from Franklin take pride in creating a comfortable and inviting atmosphere, and their warm greetings reflect their commitment to making people feel valued and respected in their community.

Polite Language

Politeness is highly valued. While Franklin has a progressive feel to it, the use of "sir" and "ma'am" is a common way to show respect, regardless of age. We use polite language such as "please" and "thank you" in everyday conversations. In Franklin, we're courteous and respectful in our communication. We prioritize manners and politeness in our interactions, avoiding confrontational or offensive language. The use of polite language reflects a commitment to hospitality, good manners, and creating a positive and respectful atmosphere in social interactions. It is a cultural value that underscores the importance of treating others with kindness and consideration.

Eye Contact

Maintaining eye contact while conversing is a sign of attentiveness and respect. It's seen as a way to show that you're fully engaged in the conversation, value the other person's presence, and have nothing to hide. Maintaining eye contact during a conversation is a sign of respect and attentiveness. In Southern culture, making eye contact fosters a sense of trust and connection between individuals. It helps establish rapport and sincerity in interactions, conveying confidence, sincerity, and honesty. Southerners appreciate clear and open communication, and eye contact is a part of that. In many Southern communities, including Franklin, maintaining eye contact is simply a social norm.

Hospitality

Southern hospitality is a hallmark of Franklin's manners. Inviting neighbors, friends, and even newcomers into one's home for meals, gatherings, or just a friendly chat is a common practice. Hospitality is important in Franklin, Tennessee, because it embodies our culture of warmth, courtesy, and neighborliness. It's a way to make others feel valued and welcome, whether it's through offering a friendly greeting or providing a helping hand. Hospitality is a cornerstone of Southern identity because it reflects the community's commitment to building strong relationships and creating an inviting and inclusive environment for all.

Helping Neighbors

Franklin residents often go out of their way to help their neighbors. It isn't nosy here (or creepy) to volunteer to assist with yard work, lend tools, offer to carpool children to and from school, or offer a helping hand during [perceived] difficult times. And if you "overstep" a boundary, it's forgivable. Helping neighbors is crucial because it embodies the culture of community, support, and reciprocity. Southerners place high value on strong bonds with their neighbors, viewing them as extended family. Offering assistance and kindness to neighbors in times of need is a way to uphold the tradition of Southern hospitality, ensuring that everyone feels cared for and connected. It reinforces the sense of belonging and the belief that together, the community thrives and overcomes challenges, reflecting the deeply rooted values of togetherness and mutual aid in Southern culture.

RESPECTING ELDERS

Respecting and taking care of elders is an important aspect of small town manners. Holding doors open, offering seats, and showing deference are ways of honoring the older generations. Respecting elders is paramount to us in Franklin, Tennessee, as it reflects our deeply ingrained values of tradition, family, and courtesy. Southerners place a strong emphasis on showing deference and gratitude to those who have accumulated wisdom and experience. Respecting elders is a way to preserve and honor the heritage and values passed down through generations. It also fosters a sense of community and continuity, reinforcing the belief that learning from and cherishing the insights of older generations is essential in maintaining the rich tapestry of Southern culture and family bonds.

Small Talk

Engaging in friendly small talk is a common way to build connections. Whether it's discussing the weather, local events, or family matters, these conversations help foster a sense of community. Small talk does not include political, religious, or other potentially controversial conversations. "Small talk" is important to us in Franklin, Tennessee, because it serves as a social lubricant, fostering warmth and connections. Southerners value friendly and relaxed interactions, even with strangers, as it creates a sense of community and politeness. Engaging in small talk is a way to build rapport, convey hospitality, and maintain a congenial atmosphere. It also reflects the Southern tradition of taking time to connect with others and show genuine interest in their well-being. Small talk is a bridge to deeper, more meaningful conversations and relationships.

ATTIRE

While there are a wide range of people and their clothing styles in Franklin, dressing neatly and modestly is often considered a sign of respect for oneself and others. People in Franklin tend to be mindful of their appearance, especially when attending social events. "Decent attire" is important to a Southerner from Franklin, Tennessee, as it aligns with the region's emphasis on respect, tradition, and manners. Southerners often place value on presenting themselves neatly and respectfully, especially in social and formal settings. Dressing appropriately is a way to show consideration for others, uphold cultural norms, and convey a sense of self-respect. It reflects the Southern pride in maintaining a dignified appearance, which is seen as a mark of politeness and adherence to the community's shared values and expectations.

Punctuality

It's a misnomer to believe that it is normal or acceptable in small-towns like Franklin is to be "fashionably" late. While the pace of life may be a bit slower, punctuality is still important. Being on time is a way to show that you value others' time and commitments. Punctuality is important to us because it shows that we know you're just as important as we are. It signifies respect for your time and commitments. Southerners often place a high value on courtesy and considerate behavior. Being on time is a way to show reliability and consideration for others, aligning with the region's cultural emphasis on hospitality and politeness. It reflects a commitment to maintaining harmonious relationships, as punctuality is a mark of respect for both individual schedules and collective expectations in Southern communities.

GRATITUDE

Expressing gratitude for gestures, favors, and hospitality is a fundamental aspect of these manners. A handwritten thank-you note or a verbal expression of appreciation is highly valued. Gratitude is important to people in Franklin because it reflects our culture of appreciation, humility, and strong interpersonal bonds. Southerners often express thankfulness as a way to acknowledge kindness, reinforce relationships, and uphold the values of politeness and respect. Gratitude fosters a sense of community and reinforces the belief that acknowledging the efforts and generosity of others strengthens the fabric of Southern culture. It's a way to show appreciation for the warmth and hospitality that are deeply ingrained in Southern identity and social interactions.

Inclusivity

Small town manners in Franklin emphasize inclusivity and making newcomers feel welcome. We greet new residents warmly and invite them to community events, helping them integrate into the close-knit fabric of the town. Inclusivity is important to us here, as it reflects our commitment to the values of community, hospitality, and respect. Southerners often prioritize creating a welcoming environment where everyone feels valued and included. Inclusivity aligns with the region's cultural norms of politeness and kindness, ensuring that we embrace individuals from diverse backgrounds as part of the community. We believe that a sense of togetherness and mutual support strengthens the bonds of Southern culture, promoting a harmonious and interconnected society where all are encouraged to participate and contribute.

Avoiding Conflict

While Southerners are generally polite and friendly, we also tend to avoid confrontational conversations. We often approach controversial topics such as politics or religion cautiously, if at all, because we focus on maintaining harmony. Avoiding conflict is important because it aligns with the cultural values of politeness, harmony, and community cohesion. Southerners like to maintain friendly and respectful relationships, and so we keep confrontation for a last resort. We believe in resolving differences through civil discourse and diplomacy, emphasizing the importance of keeping social interactions pleasant and constructive. Avoiding conflict reflects our commitment to preserving the warm and welcoming atmosphere in Southern communities, where individuals aim to foster goodwill, understanding, and strong social bonds.

Harlinsdale

FARM

About
SISTER CITIES

"Orange Marigold"
Tagetes erecta

Some of the best flowers for keping insects away
from your spring and summer garden.

The Sister Cities of Franklin & Williamson County share a lot of similarities that make partnerships a great fit. A sister city is a broad-based, long-term partnership between two communities in two countries. Franklin has three partnerships: County Laois, Ireland; Bad Soden, Germany; and Carleton Place, (Ontario) Canada. What follows are eighteen factors taken into consideration that make each sister city a great match.

Historic Heritage & Cultural Celebrations

Sister Cities share a common thread of historic heritage and cultural celebrations, as they forge connections rooted in shared values and traditions. These cities often commemorate their historical ties through festivals, exhibitions, and events that showcase their cultural heritage. By celebrating their shared history, they foster mutual understanding and promote cultural exchange, enriching both communities with a deeper appreciation for their common roots. This cultural bridge-building strengthens global relationships and promotes unity across borders.

Community Engagement

Sister Cities have community engagement in common through collaborative initiatives that encourage people-to-people connections. They facilitate exchanges in education, arts, and civic participation, fostering cross-cultural understanding. Residents actively engage in cultural events, youth exchanges, and volunteer programs, strengthening ties and promoting global citizenship. This shared commitment to community involvement promotes lasting friendships, enhances mutual appreciation, and helps address common challenges through shared experiences and cooperation.

Local Businesses

Sister Cities often share local business interests through economic partnerships. They collaborate on trade missions, promote investment opportunities, and facilitate commercial exchanges. Common industries and complementary strengths can lead to mutually beneficial ventures, boosting economic growth for both cities. This shared interest in business fosters a strong economic bond, encourages entrepreneurship, and creates opportunities for job creation, ultimately enhancing the prosperity and vitality of each community.

NATURAL BEAUTY

Sister Cities frequently share the natural beauty of their landscapes. Both may boast picturesque scenery, such as mountains, rivers, or coastlines, that serve as tourism magnets. These shared natural assets can inspire collaboration in eco-tourism, conservation efforts, and sustainable development. Recognizing the value of their pristine environments, Sister Cities often work together to preserve and showcase their natural beauty, attracting visitors, and fostering environmental stewardship, which in turn bolsters their local economies and enhances the quality of life for their residents.

Recreational Opportunities

Sister Cities often share recreational opportunities due to similar geographic features. Both may offer outdoor activities like hiking, biking, or water sports, thanks to their natural landscapes. This commonality can lead to collaborative initiatives in sports and leisure tourism, attracting enthusiasts from both regions. By capitalizing on their shared recreational assets, Sister Cities promote healthy lifestyles, tourism growth, and a sense of kinship through shared hobbies and interests, enriching the quality of life for their residents and visitors alike.

Sense of Community

Sister Cities often share similar values when it comes to a sense of community. They prioritize inclusivity, neighborly support, and social cohesion, fostering strong bonds among residents. These shared values promote community engagement, volunteerism, and cultural exchange, creating a sense of belonging that transcends borders. By valuing and nurturing their communities in similar ways, Sister Cities strengthen their relationships and enhance the well-being of their citizens, reinforcing the notion that we are all part of a global, interconnected family.

Local Arts & Crafts

Sister Cities frequently share a similar interest in local arts and crafts. They often exchange cultural insights, showcasing traditional art forms and crafts through exhibitions and festivals. This mutual appreciation fosters artistic collaboration, encouraging artisans and artists to learn from each other. By celebrating and supporting local creativity, Sister Cities enhance cultural enrichment and economic opportunities, preserving and promoting their unique artistic heritage while forging enduring cultural connections.

Social Issues

Sister cities with shared social issues creatively address and exchange solutions to improve their communities. Common challenges, such as housing affordability, homelessness, or public health, serve as platforms for innovative collaboration. They exchange insights, best practices, and policies, fostering collective problem-solving. For example, a city tackling homelessness might share strategies for shelters and support programs, while the other city offers expertise in affordable housing initiatives. This dynamic exchange results in improved social services, more informed policymaking, and ultimately, a higher quality of life for their residents, all while strengthening the bond of their sister city relationship.

Preservation of History

Sister Cities frequently share similar ideas about the preservation of local history. They both recognize the value of heritage and cultural identity, often collaborating on historical preservation projects, museum exchanges, and archival initiatives. This common commitment to safeguarding their past promotes a deeper appreciation for their shared history and traditions. By working together, Sister Cities ensure that their historical legacies continue to inspire and educate future generations, strengthening the bonds that connect their communities through time.

Volunteerism

Sister Cities often share similar ideas about the importance of volunteering in civic affairs. Both communities recognize that active citizen engagement is vital for social progress and community development. They promote volunteerism through joint initiatives, encouraging residents to contribute their time and skills for the betterment of society. By fostering a culture of civic participation and volunteerism, Sister Cities empower their residents to take an active role in addressing local challenges, reinforcing the belief that collective action can create positive change and strengthen the bonds between communities.

Local Cuisine

Sister Cities frequently share similar values regarding the importance of local cuisine. They celebrate their culinary heritage by exchanging recipes, hosting food festivals, and promoting traditional dishes. This mutual appreciation for local flavors preserves cultural identity while fostering culinary diplomacy. By valuing and sharing their unique cuisines, Sister Cities enhance cultural understanding and create opportunities for gastronomic exploration, enriching both communities with diverse culinary experiences and reinforcing the idea that food is a bridge to cultural exchange.

Festivals & Events

Sister Cities often share a mutual interest in hosting festivals and similar events to celebrate their local customs. They collaborate on cultural exchanges, inviting each other to participate in festivals that showcase their traditions, music, dance, and cuisine. This shared commitment to celebrating local customs promotes cross-cultural understanding, strengthens bonds, and fosters an appreciation for diversity. These vibrant events enrich the cultural fabric of both communities, creating opportunities for residents and visitors to engage in meaningful cross-cultural experiences and celebrate the richness of human heritage.

Local Government

Sister Cities often share similar ideas about local government by valuing principles of transparency, accountability, and community engagement. They may exchange best practices in governance, exploring ways to improve public services and enhance civic participation. This shared commitment to effective local governance fosters a sense of trust and responsiveness in their communities, promoting efficient administration and citizen empowerment. By aligning their values in local government, Sister Cities ensure that their residents benefit from the best practices and innovative solutions that contribute to the well-being of their communities.

Public Art

Sister Cities often share similar ideas about the importance of public art as a means of cultural expression, community identity, and civic enrichment. They collaborate on art installations, murals, and sculpture projects that beautify public spaces, tell stories, and celebrate local heritage. This shared appreciation for public art fosters creativity and community pride, creating a sense of place and belonging. By valuing and investing in public art, Sister Cities enhance their urban landscapes, engage residents and visitors, and demonstrate the power of artistic expression to unite and inspire diverse communities.

Historical Landmarks

Sister Cities often share similar ideas about the importance of local landmarks as cultural treasures and historical symbols. They collaborate to preserve and promote these iconic sites, recognizing their significance in shaping community identity and attracting tourism. This shared commitment ensures that cherished landmarks are maintained, offering educational and recreational opportunities while connecting residents to their heritage. By valuing and protecting local landmarks, Sister Cities honor their past, celebrate their uniqueness, and strengthen the ties that bind their communities through a shared sense of history and pride.

Environmental Awareness

Sister Cities often share similar ideas about the importance of environmental awareness. They collaborate on sustainability initiatives, conservation efforts, and eco-friendly practices to protect natural resources and combat climate change. This shared commitment to environmental stewardship fosters a sense of responsibility and a dedication to preserving the planet for future generations. By valuing and promoting environmental awareness, Sister Cities promote a greener, more sustainable future, and demonstrate the power of collective action in addressing global challenges.

Our Sister
CITIES

"Colorado Blue Columbine"
Aquilegia coerulea

Native to Colorado, this wildflower
has taken root in Middle Tennessee.

It is the aim of our Sister Cities program to promote peace through mutual respect, understanding, and cooperation: *one individual, one community at a time.* We established our relationship with Carleton Place, (Ontario) Canada in 2001; with County Laois, Ireland in 2008; and with Bad Soden, Germany in 2016.

CARLETON PLACE, CANADA
The Charm of Heritage and Harmony

CARLETON PLACE is a town located in eastern Ontario, Canada, along the Mississippi River. The waterway weaves a calming presence through the town, offering opportunities for boating, fishing, and leisurely walks along its banks. This natural backdrop paints an idyllic scene, particularly during the changing seasons.

A picturesque town with a strong sense of community, Carleton Place offers a mix of historic architecture, parks, and recreational facilities with the Mississippi and nearby Centennial Lake provide opportunities for boating, fishing, and other water-based activities. Carleton Place values its heritage and hosts local events that celebrate its history and culture.

Carleton Place encapsulates small-town charm and natural beauty. With a population of over 10,000, Carleton Place exudes a sense of tranquility and community that resonates with both residents and visitors.

The town's historic downtown, adorned with classic architecture and tree-lined streets, invites strolls that evoke a nostalgic ambiance. Quaint shops, local boutiques, and inviting cafes create an atmosphere that harks back to a simpler time, while still embracing modern sensibilities.

The town's commitment to preserving its history is showcased in landmarks like the Carleton Place and Beckwith Heritage Museum, where the stories of the past come to life. Carleton Place is also a hub for artisans and artists, with galleries and creative spaces contributing to its cultural tapestry.

A strong sense of community radiates through Carleton Place. Local events, from farmers' markets to festivals, foster connections among neighbors and friends. The warmth and hospitality of the residents create an inviting atmosphere that makes one feel instantly at home.

Carleton Place strikes a harmonious balance between heritage and progress, embodying the essence of a close-knit Canadian town while embracing the present. Its riverside tranquility, historic charm, and vibrant community spirit make Carleton Place a hidden gem where the rhythms of everyday life harmonize with the natural beauty that surrounds it.

COUNTY LAOIS, IRELAND
Natural Splendor and Rolling Landscapes

COUNTY LAOIS, also known as "Laois," is a county located in the province of Leinster in Ireland. It is characterized by rolling hills, farmland, and a mix of historical sites and modern developments. Laois offers a blend of rural landscapes, historic sites like the Rock of Dunamase, and cultural attractions. The county's heritage is reflected in its castles, abbeys, and traditional Irish music and dance. Laois embraces both its historical roots and its contemporary contributions to Irish culture.

County Laois exudes a captivating blend of rural tranquility and vibrant culture in the heart of Ireland. With its rolling hills, charming villages, and historical landmarks, this county weaves a tapestry of Ireland's rich heritage.

Laois's landscape paints a portrait of serene beauty. The Slieve Bloom Mountains, shrouded in mist and mystique, provide a backdrop for outdoor enthusiasts. Verdant valleys, meandering rivers like the Barrow and Nore, and lush woodlands invite exploration, offering a haven for hikers, cyclists, and nature lovers.

Historical echoes resonate through Laois's ancient sites and landmarks. The Rock of Dunamase, a dramatic ruined fortress perched high, holds stories of medieval battles and conquests. Emo Court, a neo-classical mansion, and Timahoe Round Tower, a symbol of early Christian architecture, stand as testaments to the county's diverse history.

Laois thrives on its cultural heritage. The county's traditional Irish music scene reverberates through local pubs, fostering an atmosphere of shared melodies and camaraderie. Festivals like Electric Picnic celebrate music and arts, while local events revive medieval traditions, breathing life into history.

Warmth and community spirit define Laois. Its small towns and villages radiate a sense of belonging. From the county's culinary scene that showcases local produce to its dedication to preserving Gaelic language and culture, Laois embraces its roots while embracing progress.

County Laois encapsulates Ireland's essence—a landscape where nature and history interlace, a canvas where culture and community thrive. Its landscapes and landmarks whisper tales of generations past, while its villages exude the charm of Irish rural life, and its commitment to tradition and progress embodies the heart of the Emerald Isle.

BAD SODEN AM TAUNUS, GERMANY
Cultural Riches and Natural Beauty

BAD SODEN is a spa town located in the Main-Taunus district of Hesse, Germany. It is known for its mineral springs and wellness facilities. Bad Soden is a health-oriented town with a focus on wellness and relaxation. The town's spa culture attracts visitors seeking therapeutic treatments and a tranquil environment. The surrounding Taunus Mountains provide opportunities for outdoor activities like hiking and nature exploration.

Bad Soden, cradled in Germany's Hesse region, is a captivating spa town that marries tradition with modern comfort. With a population of around 22,000, Bad Soden is known for its rejuvenating thermal springs, lush landscapes, and rich cultural heritage.

Bad Soden's historic architecture reflects its storied past. The charming Altstadt, or Old Town, exudes a nostalgic aura with its cobblestone streets, half-timbered houses, and enchanting squares. The St. Katharinenkirche, a Gothic church dating back to the 13th century, stands as a testament to the town's enduring heritage.

The town's connection to nature is integral to its identity. The Taunus mountains that frame Bad Soden offer a scenic backdrop for outdoor enthusiasts. Hiking trails, cycling routes, and verdant parks invite exploration, providing a serene escape from urban life.

Cultural enrichment thrives in Bad Soden, with galleries, museums, and music events that celebrate the arts. The Kunstforum der Stadtsparkasse Bad Soden, an art forum, showcases local and international artists, adding a touch of creativity to the town's ambiance.

Bad Soden's community spirit shines through its festivals and events. From traditional markets to music festivals, the town's residents come together to celebrate their heritage and connect with one another. The warmth of the community is palpable, welcoming both visitors and new residents with open arms.

Radnor Lake

NASHVILLE

Local Annual
EVENTS

"CRAPE MYRTLE"
Lagerstroemia

Crape myrtles make themselves known every June
with blooms that range from white to hot pink.

ART CRAWL
(DOWNTOWN FRANKLIN)
First Friday Night of the Month

KIDS ARTS FESTIVAL
(PINKERTON PARK)
March 25, 2023

ARBOR DAY
(PINKERTON PARK)
April 29, 2023

MAIN STREET FESTIVAL
(MAIN STREET)
Fourth full weekend in April

TOUCH-A-TRUCK
(JIM WARREN PARK)
Third Friday in May

FRANKLIN RODEO
(WILLIAMSON COUNTY AG EXPO PARK)
Third weekend in May

EAT THE STREET
(BICENTENNIAL PARK IN FRANKLIN)
First Friday of June

MOVIES IN THE PARK
(PINKERTON PARK)
Select Days in June & July

FRANKLIN ON THE FOURTH
(PARADE THROUGH DOWNTOWN FRANKLIN)
July 4

FIREWORKS
(FIREWORKS BEGIN AT 9 P.M.)
July 4

Bluegrass Along the Harpeth
(Franklin Square)
Fourth Weekend in July

Williamson County Fair
(4215 Long Ln Ste 100 Franklin, TN 37064)
First few days in August

Pilgrimage Festival
(The Park at Harlinsdale Farm)
The Third Weekend of September

Westhaven Porchfest
(Westhaven Community)
The Last Saturday of September/First Saturday of October
Pumpkinfest
(Downtown Franklin)
Saturday before Halloween

FAMILY DAY
(THE PARK AT HARLINSDALE FARM)
First Saturday in November

VETERANS DAY PARADE
(THE PARK AT HARLINSDALE FARM)
On or about November 11

WINE DOWN MAIN STREET
(MAIN STREET)
First Saturday in November

CHRISTMAS TREE LIGHTING CEREMONY
(PUBLIC SQUARE)
First Friday in December

FRANKLIN ROTARY
(DOWNTOWN FRANKLIN)
First Saturday in December

FLASHLIGHT CANDY CANE HUNT
(EASTERN FLANK BATTLEFIELD PARK)
First weekend in December

DICKENS OF A CHRISTMAS
(DOWNTOWN FRANKLIN)
Second Weekend in December

Cheekwood Gardens
NASHVILLE

Visionary
ORGANIZATIONS

"WINTERBERRY"
Ilex verticillata

Known for its holly berry appearance,
Winterberry grows all winter.

AMBASSADOR PROGRAM
www.visitfranklin.com/ambassador

ENVISION FRANKLIN
www.franklintn.gov

HABITAT FOR HUMANITY
WILLIAMSON-MAURY
www.hfhwm.org

LEADERSHIP FRANKLIN
www.leadershipfranklin.com

THE HERITAGE FOUNDATION
OF WILLIAMSON, TN
www.williamsonheritage.org

THE WILLIAMSON COUNTY CONVENTION
AND VISITORS BUREAU (WCCVB)
www.visitfranklin.com

WILLIAMSON INC.
www.williamsonchamber.com

The Parthenon
NASHVILLE

Jody Nash
About the Photographer

Jody Nash is a hair stylist & photographer who specializes in commercial and editorial-style photography. She is originally from Red Bud, Illinois.

As a freelance hairstylist for CMA, Nissan, and Curb Records, Jody has been published in magazines like *Country, People UK,* and *Muscle Magazine.* As a freelance photographer, Jody has a detailed and whimsical editing style that her clients find endearing, especially in her landmark photography.

The mother of two children, Jody has lived in Franklin, Tennessee for twenty-five years.

To Contact Jody Nash
jodynash2268@gmail.com
(931) 334-0809

SHARILYN GRAYSON
ABOUT THE EDITOR

SHARILYN GRAYSON is a writer, ghostwriter, and editor who has worked with a wide variety of national and international clients. She is originally from Cocoa Beach, Florida, and was raised in Charlotte, North Carolina.

After receiving a bachelor degree in Theater Education with a minor in English in 1997, Sharilyn moved to Franklin where she has lived for 25 years and worked on the editing side of publishing for 22 years. A prolific reader, Sharilyn has authored several YA books. Most notable is *Plague* and her *Dawn Hyperdrive* series.

Sharilyn is married and the mother of six children.

TO CONTACT SHARILYN GRAYSON
sharilynsuzetteedits@gmail.com

1799

Established

Additional
Acknowledgments

First & Foremost, we want to thank Eric Jacobson of the The Battle of Franklin Trust for his many recommendations on the timeline and historic site descriptions. (We took most of them).

Next, thanks goes to the board members of Sister Cities of Franklin & Williamson County. The feedback, recommendations, and edits were a superb demonstration of the collaborative spirit of Sister Cities.

Lastly, many thanks goes to civic leadership of our great community, past and present, in creating a place where so many of us from a variety of backgrounds have been able to make Franklin and Williamson County our home.

Traitmarker Media LLC is a book publishing service and advisory company in Franklin, Tennessee, that specializes in positioning author stories for social impact.

TRAITMARKER MEDIA LLC
www.traitmarkermedia.com
traitmarker@gmail.com

SISTER★CITIES
of Franklin and Williamson County
TENNESSEE

The misison of SISTER CITIES OF FRANKLIN &
WILLIAMSON COUNTY in all its endeavors
is to build global relationships, to share cultural
and educational experiences, and to inspire
the economic growth of our community.
SISTER CITIES is a 501c3 organization.

SISTER CITIES OF FRANKLIN &
WILLIAMSON COUNTY
www.sistercitiestn.org
sistercitiesfranklintn@gmail.com

Nashville
DOWNTOWN

Milton Keynes UK
Ingram Content Group UK Ltd.
UKHW051020201123
432904UK00004B/68